LAKE of GARDA

(Cover photo) Western Garda

LAKE of GARDA

INTRODUCTION

The Lake of Garda, the biggest of the Italian lakes, is famous as a Mediterranean oasis at the foot of the Alps. Here, olive trees and vines yield precious fruits, green Mediterranean vegetation covers the hillsides and orchids grow wild in the meadows and mountain pastures, like those of the impressive chain of Monte Baldo or Monte Pizzocolo, facing the lake.

The gardens of the villas are rich in exotic species which, thanks to the mild climate, have adapted perfectly to the conditions here. Lemons have been eported throughout Europe for centuries.

The waters of the Lake of Garda are rich in fish - eels, trout, bleaks, whitefish, chub, shad and many others. But these are above all the waters of the giant carp, a rare member of the salmon family with very delicate flesh which can be found only in the Lake of Garda. The lake is divided into two zones, the fjord-like area of the north and the almost maritime area of the south, below the line traced between San Vigilio Point and the Gulf of Salò. The basin covers 370 square kilometres, with a maximum width of 17.5 km and a length of around 52 km. The maximum depth is 350 metres (off Brenzone). The most important river, the Sarca, enters the lake from the north. The Mincio, which collects the waters of the lake, flows out at Peschiera. Of the islands, the most important are Garda and Trimelone.

In ancient times, the lake was known as Benàco, but the name was changed to Garda in medieval times, probably because of the strategic and military importance of the fortress on Rocca di Garda. With the beauty of its locations, its calm landscapes, mild climate, historic

memories, natural heritage and renowned hospitality, the Lake of Garda is the destination of many thousands of visitors each year, following in the footsteps of famous travellers from every era, enchanted by the blue landscapes of Garda - Virgil, Catullus, Dante, Goethe, Carducci, Lawrence, Kafka, D'Annunzio and many others have composed verses or waxed lyrical over the beauties of the area.

Because of its particularly favourable environmental and climatic features, the Garda area has been populated since remote times, as a large number of very important archaeological finds prove. Entire villages of lake dwellings have been brought to light throughout the southern part of the lake. On the first rocky contours of the north eastern part of the riviera, there are thousands of inscriptions that tell the tale of four thousand years of history.

As an essential area of passage between the Po plain and central Europe, Garda was disputed by dominions and armies. It was an area claimed by different peoples, and various works of art have been found on the banks which testify to the evolution of European culture in the course of the centuries. The Roman and Lombard remains are especially fascinating. Scaligers, Venetians and Visconti erected walls and castles that give the modern visitor the opportunity of exploring the past. During the Renaissance, splendid palaces belonging to noble families fascinated by the Garda area flourished. In the nineteenth century, Austrian military engineers constructed massive defence complexes. Then, it was the turn of modern tourism. The villas of the first central European visitors sprang up, and the first hotels were built. Today, the Lake of Garda is one of the leading tourist zones of Europe, with over two million visitors spending their holidays here each year.

CONTENTS

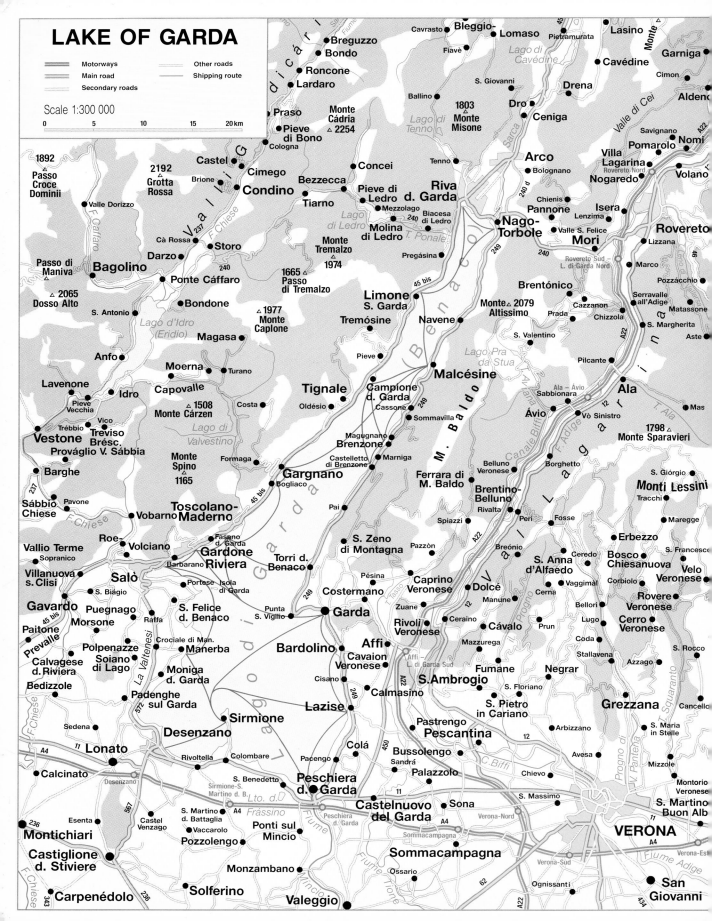

LAKE OF GARDA

Motorways
Main road
Secondary roads
Other roads
Shipping route

Scale 1:300 000

0   5   10   15   20 km

Sirmione

A century before the birth of Christ, the Latin poet Caius Valerius Catullus described Sirmione as the pearl of the islands and peninsulas. And Sirmione is still a true pearl of Garda, a green peninsula that stretches out towards the pale blue of the lake, a three-kilometre long strip of land jutting out into the southern basin of Benàco.

Sirmione is well known as a resort with a mild climate, a zone rich in history and a health spa. The Boiola spring has been known since ancient times, but it has been systematically used only since 1889, when its thermal waters were channelled into pipes from the bed of the lake. In 1921 the Terme Grandi Alberghi company was founded in Sirmione, marking the start of the modern fortunes of the area.

Without exaggerating, however, we can say that Sirmione has been a resort for centuries. The large Roman villa on the buttress where the peninsula of Sirmione ends is thought to have belonged to Catullus, though in fact the poet was the guest of Sirmione (where he also ended his days). But the so-called Catullus Grottoes very probably had no connection with him, due to their vastness and the almost certainty that most of this extraordinary Roman architectural complex was built after his death.

However, we can be sure that a visit to the monumental Roman ruins of Sirmione has all the fascination of a trip back in time. Here, every corner has something to say on the history of the lake.

For example, the times of the Lombards are reflected in the very old church of San Pietro in Mavino, rebuilt at the start of the 14th century, rich in frescoes from various eras. Not far off, we find the recently constructed Campana dei Caduti, which invokes peace in the world.

The castle with the fine embattlements facing the lake is one of the most beautiful in Italy.

It testifies to the great strategic and military importance of Sirmione. From the keep - 47 metres - we can fully appreciate this magnificent defensive structure built by the Scaligers.

Page 5
Sirmione, the inner basin
of the Rocca Scaligera

Sirmione, the imposing fortification
of the fortress seen from the entrance
to the town centre

Sirmione, the lively Piazza Carducci

Sirmione, view of the town centre
from the Rocca Scaligera

Near the fortress is the little church of Sant'Anna (14th century), with an interesting series of devotional frescoes. The parish church of Santa Maria Maggiore dates back to the 15th century, contains a Eucharist Supper painted by Paolo Farinati and has a series of interesting sixteenth century frescoes.

Many visitors to Sirmione take interest in the villa opposite the Villa Cortine Hotel where the great opera singer Maria Callas lived in the fifties, and who is well remembered in Sirmione.

Sirmione, the Scaliger Fortress by night

Sirmione, Festa dell'Ospite, fireworks display

Sirmione, view of the Roman remains of the "Catullus Grottoes"

*Below, Sirmione,
Church of San Pietro in Mavino*

Sirmione, "Catullus Grottoes"

Sirmione, "Catullus Grottoes" from the lake

Desenzano

The town of Desenzano is one of the most important and busiest centres on the Lake of Garda. Here, we find traces of very old settlements, with the remains of a number of lake dwellings dated to the Early Bronze Age, the period of the prehistoric civilisation known as Polada, which takes its name from an area between Desenzano and Lonato where important archaeological discoveries were made from the second half of the nineteenth century onwards.

The Roman era is represented by the villa - attributed to the third or fourth century AD - near the centre of Desenzano, whose remains were discovered in 1921. Some fine mosaic floors, among the most important of those discovered in northern Italy, are well conserved, with hunting and fishing scenes together with geometric figures, cupids and allegories. The interesting finds from the archaeological zone of Borgo Regio can be seen in the Antiquarium adjacent to the Roman villa, and include amphoras, sculptures, bronze tools and lamps.

Positioned in a garden is the sarcophagus of Attilia Ubrica, in white stone, also from Roman times, perhaps the 3rd century AD. Important structures remain of the medieval castle, though modified in the course of the centuries. Fine views may be had over the lake. The quadrangular tower was the original bell tower.

Desenzano, the characteristic old port with the porticoes of the Provveditore palace

Desenzano, the basin, pier with lighthouse

In Venetian times, the port of Desenzano was the most important market of the area, an important trading centre, but there was also smuggling, strongly persecuted by the Venetian authorities.

At that time, there emerged two works of architecture by Giulio Todeschini (1524-1603) - the palace of the Provveditore, with a fine portico facing on to the old basin, and the parish church of Santa Maria Maddalena, with three naves and an excellent Last Supper by Giambattista Tiepolo along with other important paintings by Andrea Celesti, Zenon Veronese and others. In the sacristy there is a Pietà by Palma il Giovane. The canvas also shows Sant'Angela Merici (1474-1540), founder of the Ursulines and a native of Desenzano, also commemorated by a marble statue in Piazza Malvezzi, near the port. Another interesting monument in Desenzano is the one in honour of the Flying Squad, which was active in the town from 1927 to 1936. One of its members was Marshall Francesco Agello, who broke the world speed record for hydroplanes on the Lake of Garda. The former fifteenth century convent of Santa Maria di Senioribus now contains a library and museum dedicated to the prehistoric period.

The poet Angelo Anelli (1761-1820), friend of Gioacchino Rossini and author of the libretto "The Italian in Algiers", is a native of Desenzano.

The village of Rivoltella has an interesting church, known as San Zeno, with interesting seventeenth century stuccoes. In San Martino della Battaglia, on a hill set in the green countryside, there is a 64 metre tower commemorating the Risorgimento battle of 1859. Alongside the tower are the museum and charnel-house.

Desenzano, aerial view

Desenzano, the promenade

Desenzano, town centre, with castle in the background

*Desenzano, promenade,
port and monument
to the Flying Squad*

Desenzano, the old port

Desenzano, promenade and lighthouse

Desenzano, Roman villa, the multicoloured floor mosaics

San Martino della Battaglia, tower and charnel-house

La Valtenesi

La Valtenesi, which stretches from the riviera to the morainic hills formed by glaciers in the remote past, deserves attention not only for its landscape and history, but also for the delicious local produce, such as excellent oil and top quality wines such as Chiaretto and Groppello. This area, dominated by the green of the vines and olive trees, comprises Padenghe, Moniga, Soiano, Polpenazze, Puegnago, Manerba, San Felice and Portese.

One of the many legends of the Lake of Garda and the surrounding areas, with their long history, tells that refugees from Athens in ancient times found hospitality here. The myth was later taken up by Carducci, and leads to the traditional notion that the name of Valtenesi derives from Vallis Atheniensis.

Undoubtedly, the area has been inhabited since prehistoric times, as

The wide southern gulf from the hills of Valtenesi

Panorama

The medieval castle of Moniga

demonstrated by the archeological finds on the shores of the lake (remains of lake dwellings at Manerba and San Felice), in the immediate surroundings (in the fortress of Manerba, for example, whose finds, together with others from the surrounding area, are on display in the small museum in the parish church) and inland, especially in the fascinating lakelet area of Sovenigo, not far from Puegnago, and the former lake of Lucone, now reclaimed, near Polpenazze (the mould of a pirogue found here is displayed with other finds in the museum of Gavardo). In the course of the centuries, many small forts were built in Valtenesi, with significant remains in Padenghe, with the castle overlooking the lake and the valley, in Moniga where the medieval walls surround part of the village, and also in Soiano.

Manerba

Manerba. The impressive gulf with the fortress in the background

Manerba. The characteristic profile of the fortress and the other islands seen from above

From the Fortress of Manerba, once an important strategic point, we gaze over the Lake of Garda.

This is one of the most interesting landscapes of the lake for its extraordinary variety of vegetation. Important prehistoric remains were found here by archaeologists.

Among the works of art, we should mention the Pieve di Santa Maria in Valtenesi (12th-13th centuries), in Romanesque style.

Isola del Garda

The Isola del Garda (a kilometre long) was also known as Lecchi, Ferrari and Borghese, from the names of the families that owned it, and Isola dei Frati due to the monastery founded there, probably by Saint Francis of Assisi in 1220, which later became a theological centre. Today, built in a magnificent park, is a splendid villa, inspired by Venetian Gothic style and built between 1894 and 1901.

Isola del Garda. Villa Cavazza set in the splendid park

Isola del Garda. The luxuriant vegetation

Salò

The small town of Salò, referred to in ancient documents with the name of Salodium, faces onto a bright bay, protected by Monte San Bartolomeo. It is situated among the morainic hills of western Garda where vines and olive trees are grown, and surrounded by the typical vegetation of the Mediterranean.

Salò was also a capital in the past. Firstly, during the Venetian period, it was the centre of the Magnifica Patria and was also known, with pride, as the Riviera di Salò, with authority over the centres of the west bank of the lake. Then, for a short time, from 1943 to 1945, it was the headquarters of the ill-fated Italian Social Republic, founded on the shores of the Lake of Garda by Benito Mussolini.

Salò is rich in historical and artistic memories, starting from the cathedral, a Gothic-Renaissance masterpiece. Work beg—an on this in 1453, but it remained unfinished, as we can see from the brick façade, which never received its facing. However, the marble doorway, attributed to Antonio della Porta and Gasparo da Cairano, is most interesting. Inside, there are three naves. There is a fifteenth century wooden crucifix, the work of a certain Johannes Teutonichus, and much admired by Andrea Mantegna. There is an extraordinary series of paintings by Andrea Celesti, Palma il Giovane (also responsible for the evangelists in the cupola and the paintings on the doors of the splendid organ), Gerolamo Romanino, Paolo Veneziano, Giovanni Battista Trotti known as Malosso, perhaps also Moretto or Torbido, and finally Zenon Veronese, who also has other works in Salò, in the churches of San Giovanni and San Bernardino.

Among the civil buildings, we should mention the architectural complex of the Magnifica Patria and Town Hall building on the promenade, with its fine portico. The town hall, of sixteenth century origins - designed by Sansovino - was rebuilt at the start of the twentieth century.

Salò, the colourful gulf

Salò, the long promenade

From the Magnifica Patria building, justice was administered to the inhabitants of west Garda during Venetian times. Today, the building houses an archaeological museum with important Roman remains.

There remain interesting traces of the medieval walls. Also well preserved is the clock tower, a point of access to the town (La Porta della Rocca).

In the village of Barbarano, there is the sixteenth century Martinengo-Terzi palace built by the Marquis Sforza Pallavicino.

Gasparo Bertolotti, known as Gasparo da Salò (1540-1609) was born in Salò. He is believed to be the inventor of the violin, based on the older soprano viola. The Athenaeum of Salò, containing a rich and prestigious library, dates from the sixteenth century. There is also a meteorological observatory, founded at the end of the nineteenth century.

Salò, panorama

Salò, the gulf from Villa Portesina

Salò, the cathedral, Gothic-Renaissance façade

Salò, the cathedral. Interior with the main altar

Gardone Riviera

The history of tourism in Gardone Riviera is longer than that of many other resorts on the lake. It was in the second half of the nineteenth century that the German engineer Ludwig Wimmer started the modern tourist age. Wimmer arrived in Gardone to convalesce, and in 1874 decided to stay. In 1881 he became mayor of the town. He publicized the town in Germany and built the Grand Hotel in 1883 to host his fellow nationals.

Later, other hotels were built, along with the casino and magnificent villas (for example, Villa Alba, in neoclassical style, with a fine colonnade) in Gardone and nearby Fasano. Some of the villas hosted important figures from the Republic of Salò during the second world war. In Villa Fiordaliso in Gardone there was Claretta Petacci, the Japanese ambassador lived in Villa Turati, also in Gardone, and the German Embassy was housed in Villa Cristofori, in Fasano.

Gardone became famous abroad as a holiday and health resort, with the founding of several clinics such as Villa Primavera of Doctor Koeniger, who has left us many details on the local climate from 1885 onwards, sufficient to promote Gardone to first place among the climatic resorts of northern Italy.

New plant species, often exotic, were gradually brought into the parks surrounding the villas. These quickly adapted to the local climate and blended in with the spontaneous Mediterranean vegetation. An admirable example of the extraordinary botanical heritage of Gardone is the gardens created by Arturo Hruska. The Hruska Botanic Garden was founded in 1910 and contains Mediterranean, exotic and alpine vegetation in a vast array of shapes and colours. This confirms the fortunate position of Gardone.

In this way, then, tourism has evolved in Gardone since the end of the nineteenth century. The oldest known history of the area tells us that there must have been a settlement here in Roman times, borne out by several tombstones, classified by Mommsen. In the Venetian period, Gardone belonged to the territory of the Magnifica Patria, and its praises were sung by poets and visitors alike. Today, Gardone Riviera contains the headquarters of the Comunità del Garda, an association comprising all the local governments around the lake.

Among the works of art, we should mention the eighteenth century parish church, built on the foundations of an older church, and the Romanesque church of Morgnaga, dedicated to St. Anthony Abbott and containing a wooden triptych of Sant'Emiliano with two other saints.

Gardone Riviera.
The basin and the exclusive promenade

Gardone Riviera.The promenade and
the Grand Hotel seen from the boat

*Gardone Riviera. The lush Mediterranean
vegetation on the promenade*

Gardone Riviera by night, from above

*Gardone Riviera.
The Hruska Botanical Garden*

*Gardone Riviera.
The parish church of San Nicola*

Il Vittoriale degli Italiani

Gabriele D'Annunzio first visited Villa Cargnacco, in the hills of Gardone Riviera, in 1921, and remained there for seventeen years, until his death. Before D'Annunzio, the villa belonged to the German art critic Henry Thode, related to the families of Wagner and Liszt, and before him it was owned by the widow of Ludwig Wimmer, the first promoter of tourism in Gardone. D'Annunzio arranged for the complete restoration of the property, commissioning the architect Gian Carlo Maroni. Villa Cargnacco and its grounds was soon transformed into Il Vittoriale degli Italiani. Every year, thousands of tourists visit this house-museum of the famous poet, which has long been associated with important artists and personalities.

The home of D'Annunzio was the Priory. The various rooms, which fascinate the visitor for the enormous quantity of objects of various origins to be found there, bear the names the poet gave them in accordance with elaborate symbols (The Room of the Maskmaker, Leda, Leper, the Verandah of Apollino and so on to the Workshop, the study of D'Annunzio).

In the upper part of the park we find the Mausoleum, designed by Maroni after the death of the poet to lay his remains and those of ten legionaries of Fiume. Among the cypresses, lower down, is the ship "Puglia", an unusual monument. The park also has an open-air theatre, in a setting of great beauty. The theatre is inspired by the Greek style and excellent performances are staged here every year. In the Auditorium, the plane that flew over Vienna is suspended from the ceiling.

Gardone Riviera, Il Vittoriale, façade of the Mausoleum

Gardone Riviera, Il Vittoriale, Mausoleum with D'Annunzio's Tomb

Gardone Riviera, Il Vittoriale, open-air theatre with broad view over the Lake of Garda

Gardone Riviera, Il Vittoriale, façade of the Priory

Gardone Riviera, Il Vittoriale, the ship "Puglia"

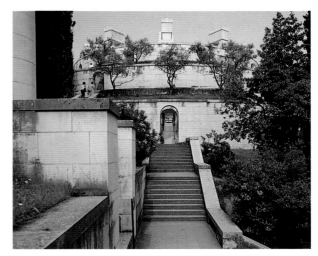

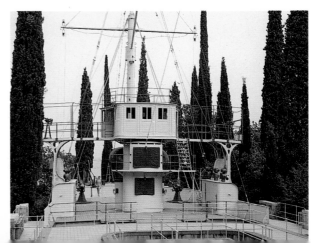

Fasano

Fasano, panorama from the hillside

Maderno

32

Maderno, the promenade

Maderno, Church of Sant'Andrea

Maderno, boats moored in the harbour

Maderno, cypresses on the shore

The harmony of the Gulf of Maderno, among the green Mediterranean vegetation, is suddenly revealed to those approaching the lake, perhaps on board the ferry that goes from here to Torri del Benaco. This is where the Gonzaga family, rulers of Mantua, had their lakeside residence.

Maderno contains one of the most interesting architectural sites of Garda - the old church of Sant'Andrea, an elegant example of the Romanesque style, built around the 12th century, though some experts say it may date back to the 9th century. Ancient chronicles state that the church was built on the foundations of a pagan temple. Those who maintain this theory say that this can be proven by much material found in Roman buildings set in the outer walls. The crypt contained the sarcophagus of Sant'Ercolano. The relics, which, according to tradition, were the subject of bitter disputes between the inhabitants of Maderno and those of nearby Toscolano, were transferred to the current parish church in 1825, where there are also a number of paintings, including Sant'Ercolano at prayer from the school of Paolo Caliari, known as Il Veronese (1528-1588).

Toscolano

According to legend, there once existed a town named Benàco, which was plummeted into the waters of the lake by a cataclysm. And tradition says that this was built on the site of the modern town of Toscolano.

The legend probably originates from the archeological finds in Toscolano from the Roman period. The remains of an imposing Roman villa were brought to light near the parish church. There may have been two pagan temples in the ancient Toscolano, with Christian churches built on their foundations. The modern church dedicated to Saints Peter and Paul is built on the site where once the praises of Bacchus were sung, and here we can find around twenty important works by the Venetian painter Andrea Celesti (1637-1712). On the site of the temple of Zeus Amon - the columns still remain today - the sanctuary of the Madonna of Benàco is built.

Toscolano was well known for its prestigious printing presses and paper works, now interesting examples of "industrial archaeology" along the valley of the Toscolano stream.

Toscolano. Parish church of Saints Peter and Paul

Toscolano. The characteristic port

Bogliaco

There are many aristocratic villas, often with splendid parks, along the shores of the Lake of Garda. Among these, one of the most important is the eighteenth century palace of the Counts Bettoni in Bogliaco, with an extraordinary garden designed by Amerigo Vincenzo Pierallini, with rococoes and sculptures by Domenico Cignaroli.

Since 1951, Bogliaco has been the headquarters of the Centomiglia, the most important international freshwater regatta.

Bogliaco. The imposing eighteenth century façade and Italian style garden of Palazzo Bettoni

Gargnano

In Gargnano we enter the world of the ancient lemon groves of the Lake of Garda, now virtually a memory, from the times when the "model lemon" was produced here and exported throughout Europe. There are a few fine villas on the shore of the lake, such as Feltrinelli, the home of Benito Mussolini at the time of the Republic of Salò. The landscape and people of Gargnano are well documented in the diary of the English writer D.H. Lawrence.

This is also the starting place of the "Meandro", the northern part of the west Garda road, dug out of the rock for Gabriele D'Annunzio on the design of Riccardo Cozzaglio.

Gargnano. A view of the lower part of the lake

Gargnano, the promenade

Gargnano, the basin in the centre of the town

Western
Garda

Tignale and Tremosine

The territory of Tignale stretches from the Garda riviera, with its port and beaches, to the plateau where it overlooks the lake. Because of its strategic position, it was disputed for centuries by all those interested in controlling the area. The first inhabitants of the plateau were, according to tradition, the Cenomani Gauls, who erected small pagan temples dedicated to the Benàco gods.

Today, in Tignale, the Sanctuary of Madonna di Montecastello rises sheer from the lake at a height of nearly seven hundred metres. Some say this dates back to the ninth century, and it contains a fresco that is said to belong to the school of Giotto (probably by Veronese artists) and four scenes from the Nativity of the Virgin attributed to Palma il Giovane.

Another plateau village overlooking Garda is Tremosine. The area is dotted with around twenty small centres set among meadows and woods, with sunny wooden balconies facing the lake. The administrative centre is Pieve and it is said that one of the first sites of Christian worship in the area was situated here.

On the shores of the lake, in the territory of Tignale, the famous lemon conservatory of Prato della fame is situated, a huge and ancient lemon hothouse restructured and restored to working life by the Comunità Montana Alto Garda Bresciano.

Along the road, we also reach Campione, up to a few decades ago an isolated but flourishing textile manufacturing centre.

P. 38-39.
Western Garda, fantastic views over the lake

Tignale, the typical lemon conservatories

Tignale, Sanctuary of the Madonna di Montecastello

Tignale, the sanctuary clinging to the rocks overlooking the lake

Tremosine, typical balcony overlooking the lake

A view of the Lake of Garda at the start of the Valley of Tremosine

Limone

Perhaps it was coincidence or destiny that decided that the village of Limone should take the name of the fruit that was to be cultivated there some centuries afterwards. Lemons were, in fact, grown here in the past in enormous, monumental hothouses, evidence of which still remains today (citrus production possibly began in the 13th century thanks to the efforts of the Franciscans). And yet, the name of the village derives not from the fruit, but from the term "limen", which means "border" (in the period when the territories of the Rhaeti and inhabitants of Benàco met), or from "lima", meaning pond or river (the lake or stream at Limone).

When citrus production ceases, extra virgin olive oil of excellent quality takes over as the dominant agricultural product. Among the remains of the lemon hothouses and amid the modern olive groves, we find the hotels that have made Limone one of the most important tourist centres of the Lake of Garda.

Among local artistic and historical memory, we can mention the house - now transformed into a museum - where Monsignor Daniele Comboni (1831-1881) was born - missionary bishop in Africa, founder of the Combobian Missionary Institute, the small church of San Rocco, built in 1436, with sixteenth century frescoes and the seventeenth century parish church, dedicated to San Benedetto, built on the foundations of an older church probably dating from before the 11th century and containing two large paintings by Andrea Celesti as well as a number of works by the local painter Antonio Moro (1820-1899).

An interesting scientific curiosity is the fact that some of the inhabitants of Limone have been identified as carriers of a special, very rare protein which acts as a kind of "elixir of life", highly effective against arteriosclerosis and heart disease.

Limone, impressive plays of light on Garda

Limone, the lush vegetation with the typical lemon hothouses

The olive tree, typical of the ancient traditions of Garda

Limone, the picturesque harbour

Riva. Panorama of the jetty

Riva

Riva del Garda, at the top of the Benàco, the area known as Sommolago in Venetian times, is the crossroads of the zone, with the western road dug out of the rock and the eastern road that runs along the foot of Monte Baldo, the roads for Valle del Sarca and Giudicarie. From Riva, or more accurately from Monte Brione, which rises between the town and the mouth of the Sarca river the eye ranges over a long fjord, set in the rocky slopes that form the northern part of the lakeside. Here we can see all the fascination of Garda, a pearl of the Mediterranean on the edge of the Alps.

Riva del Garda has ancient origins, as testified by several archaeological finds. This area was once under Roman domination, and an inscription refers to the existence in Roman times of a Sailing School, which shows how important this port was even then, defended from the 13th century on by the Apponale Tower, at whose summit we find Anzolim de la Tor, the tin statue of an angel which was to become the symbol of the town. The buildings in the town square (the 15th century town hall building is particularly elegant) are in Scaliger or Venetian style. The civic museum sums up the entire history of Riva and its artistic heritage, with many objects from every era, displayed in the fortress with the four corner towers. The fortress, square in shape and surrounded by a moat, was first mentioned in the 12th century. It was extended by the Scaligers, modified by the Venetians, altered by the bishop princes of Trent and transformed into an Austrian barracks in the nineteenth century.

The church-sanctuary of Inviolata, with its octagonal plan, marks the dividing line between the centre and outskirts. It was built on the site of a holy image of the Madonna, believed to have miraculous powers, painted by Mangiavino of Salò in a niche in the wall of a county estate. Inside, we can admire stuccoes by Davide Reti, frescoes by Teofilo Polacco, and three altar pieces by Palma il Giovane. The eighteenth century church of Santa Maria Assunta contains paintings by Cignaroli and Craffonara, a local painter, the creator of the altarpiece dedicated to the Assunta above the main altar. The church of Disciplina has had a curious destiny, gradually decaying and finally transformed into a connecting road towards the new areas of the town.

A few kilometres from Riva, visitors will be fascinated by the spectacular Varone waterfall, described by Thomas Mann.

Inland from Garda in the region of Trent, we find Arco, dominated by a castle perched on the cliffs and a famous health resort for the Central European aristocracy in the second half of the nineteenth century. The seventeenth century collegiate church is magnificent.

46

Riva, the fortress and inner basin

Riva, the first light of dawn on the bay

Riva, Church of Assunta

Riva, the dark gorge of the Varone waterfall

*Riva, view of the lake,
Apponale Tower in the background*

Torbole

When, on 12th December 1786, Johann Wolfgang Goethe, the great German poet and writer, leaned over the rocky slopes above Torbole, he discovered the Lake of Garda, a magnificent natural phenomenon, as he wrote in his "Italienische Reise".

He regretted not having his friends nearby to share this sudden revelation with them. At this point, he abandoned his original plan to head directly for Verona, and decided to remain at Torbole, which at that time was a poor village of fishermen, with a few houses built around the quay, not far from where the River Sarca flows down into the fjord hewn out by the glaciers to create the Lake of Garda.

Today, Torbole is a well known tourist resort. The constant winds have transformed the area into a paradise for sailing and windsurfing enthusiasts.

The harbour is still tiny, and the little house that was perhaps the office of the Venetian excise is still there. Behind, we can see the town centre, with the church of Sant'Andrea, containing a precious eighteenth century painting by Cignaroli, the Martyrdom of St. Andrew.

The centre of Torbole is dominated by the ragged cliff on which the ruins of Castel Penede are situated. This was once one of the symbols of the grandeur of the Counts of Arco. Today only a few ruins remain, but the walk towards the site is interesting, if nothing else for the magnificent views.

The village of Nago is also involved in the history of Castel Penede, with a precious sixteenth wooden statue of the Trinity in the seventeenth century church.

Along the road that leads from Torbole upwards towards Nago, it's worth stopping to admire the Marmitte dei Giganti, natural cavities (also known as "glacial wells"), created by the action of the melt waters from the ancient glaciers against the rock walls.

Torbole, impressive inscription in Goethe's lakeside residence

Torbole, the promenade

Torbole, view from above

Northern Garda from Monte Stivo

Malcesine

Among the most important tourist centres of Garda, Malcesine is situated at the foot of Monte Baldo, known for centuries as "Hortus Europae", the "botanical garden of Europe", for the richness of its flora (some flower species have the botanical name "baldensis"). Baldo is reached by cable-car from Malcesine, with a journey of only a few minutes from the riviera to the summits (Tratto Spino), with their winter ski slopes.

The centre of Malcesine, with its narrow paved streets, is dominated by the profile of the Scaliger castle, a remnant of Venetian and Austrian military engineering, which today houses a museum. On the promenade, the Palazzo dei Capitani was the residence of the Captain of the Lake, the senior Venetian official on the eastern bank of the lake. The parish church contains a fine painting by Girolamo Dai Libri, a Deposition from the 16th century.

Malcesine and the nearby village of Cassone were immortalised by the Austrian painter Gustav Klimt.

Above Cassone is the hermitage of Saints Benigno and Caro, which can be reached by a long but pleasant walk. The Aril, the shortest river in the world, around a hundred metres, flows through Cassone.

The islands are impressive - Val di Sogno e dell'Olivo and the once fortified islet of Trimelone, opposite Assenza di Brenzone.

*Malcesine,
the imposing profile of
Castello Scaligero*

*Malcesine,
the town centre and basin*

*Malcesine,
the Scaliger Castle
from the lake*

*Malcesine, looking towards
the Upper Garda*

*Malcesine, the brilliant
colours of the windsurfs*

*Malcesine,
the Monte Baldo cable-car*

Brenzone and Torri del Benaco

The territory of Brenzone counts sixteen villages scattered over the riviera of Garda, with its highly active sailing clubs, and Monte Baldo (there are cable-car installations in Prada for the summits and skilifts for Costabella, operating in winter). At Castelletto di Brenzone, the church of Santo Zeno is an important example of Romanesque art. Also at Castelletto, we can see the house of the Piccole Suore della Sacra Famiglia, an order founded by Giuseppe Nascimbeni (1851-1922).

Torri del Benàco contains a fascinating ethnographic museum, inside the Scaliger castle (14th century), dedicated to the traditions of Garda and professional fishing.

The monumental lemon hothouse can also be visited. This was built in the eighteenth century and situated against the castle. The town centre conserves its fortified medieval structure. The harbour is possibly of Roman origin. In the area, on rock slabs in the woods, there is a rich heritage of rock paintings, probably dating to the last four millenia of history.

Near Torri are Pai and Albisano, the first on the riviera among the olive trees, and the latter forming a balcony overlooking the lake.

Ski slopes on Monte Baldo, in the territory of Brenzone

Torri del Benàco, the Scaliger castle

Torri del Benàco, centre with lakeside promenade

Torri del Benàco, view of the harbour

Punta San Vigilio

A true marvel of nature and man's ingenuity, Punta San Vigilio is undoubtedly one of the most renowned and romantic corners of Italy. With its cypress-lined avenue, the Brenzoni-Guarienti palace designed by the great architect Michele Sanmicheli for Agostino Brenzoni in the sixteenth century, the Italian style garden, the small harbour with the church reflected in the waters of the lake, the blue Baia delle Sirene - these are some of the most photographed of all the sights by the tourists in the Lake of Garda.

In the exclusive inn near the harbour, reached by a lane full of inscriptions in Latin, in accordance with humanist tastes, princes and kings, actors and statesmen have stayed - Winston Churchill, Laurence Olivier and Vivien Leigh, and Prince Charles to name but a few of the visitors to Punta San Vigilio in the last few decades.

Punta San Vigilio, the enchanting Baia delle Sirene

Punta San Vigilio, sunset over the promontory

Punta San Vigilio, Villa Guarienti with the small basin

Punta San Vigilio from the lake

Garda

The Gulf of Garda is tucked between Monte Luppia to the north, with its green Mediterranean vegetation, and the fortress to the south. The medieval stronghold played such an important political and military role that the entire lake began to be known as Garda rather than the ancient Benàco from the 8th century onwards.

An ancient fishing port, with extremely proud traditions still living on - the fishermen have formed a cooperative - Garda has become one of the tourist capitals of the lake. The parish church with its ancient cloisters should be visited. The harbour square, with the Captains' Palace, is impressive, and a visit should also be paid to the elegant villa of the Counts Albertini.

On the hills inland from the lake, Costermano contains a large German military cemetery. The magnificent eighteenth century palace of the Counts Pellegrini is situated in Castion.

Garda, the gulf from
Rocca di Garda

Garda, the lodge
of the Carlotti Palace

Garda, the fortress from the harbour

Garda, the elegant Villa Albertini

Garda, the picturesque centre
with the Captains' Palace

Garda, boats at the pier

Bardolino

The name of Bardolino is undoubtedly associated with its traditional winemaking activities. In the countryside around this resort on the eastern riviera of Garda, one of the best known of Italian wines is produced, Bardolino, with its ruby red colour. The traditional grape festival takes place on the last Sunday in September.

Artistically speaking, the Bardolino area offers various testimonies to the Romanesque architectural style, starting from the church of San Severo (built between the 9th and 12th centuries), containing a fascinating cycle of frescoes, and continuing with San Pietro, on the way to Garda, San Vito in the hills and the parish church of Santa Maria, in the village of Cisano. San Zeno, built no later than the 9th century, is in Carolingian style. On the citadel is the Camaldolite hermitage, a cloister for men, with women visitors not admitted.

Bardolino, the Romanesque church of San Severo

Bardolino, the basin with the town hall

Bardolino, aerial view

Lazise

The centre of Lazise, a town which had the honour of being one of the first free communes in Italy thanks to the concessions of the emperor Otto in 983, remains inside the ancient walls built by the Scaligers and reinforced by the Venetians, who used the town as a centre of power over the markets and ports of Garda. In the harbour, where a small Venetian fleet was stationed, is the Venetian customs-house, today used for conferences, exhibitions and concerts, and the small Romanesque church of San Nicolò (12th century). The Scaliger castle is in the vicinity.

Among the events that take place in Lazise, we should mention the Certamen Catullianium, a competition for composition in Latin, and festivals dedicated to honey.

In the Bor area of the nearby village of Pacengo, there are imposing remains of a lake dwelling dating from the Bronze Age in a shallow part of the lake (various finds from here and other areas of Garda are on display in the Natural History Museum of Verona).

*Lazise, Evening light
on the harbour*

Lazise, entrance from the lake

Lazise, entrance to the surrounding walls

Lazise, Castello Scaligero from the lake

Peschiera

Peschiera is situated at the point where the Lake of Garda's waters pour into the River Mincio. The area has been inhabited since prehistoric times, as testified by various archaeological finds. It was an important Roman centre, known as Arilica. Today, it tells the story of the armies that successively took over control of the Garda territory.

The city is remembered above all for its strategic and military importance by Dante Alighieri in the "Divine Comedy". Imposing reminders of Scaliger, Venetian, Austrian, and Italian fortifications are to be found throughout tha area.

Above all, there are extraordinary examples of Austrian military engineering, which transformed the town into one of the "angles" of the Quadrilateral, the defensive system created in Lombardy-Veneto after 1815 (including Peschiera, Verona, Mantua and Legnago).

The sanctuary of Madonna del Frassino is a visitors' favourite. This was built on the site of a miraculous apparition of 1511. It contains works by Paolo Farinati (1522-1606). At Castelnuovo del Garda, a winemaking centre (Bardolino and Bianco di Custoza), there is the Gardaland amusement park. From Peschiera, we reach Valeggio sul Mincio, with its famous gastronomic traditions and an important bridge, the Scaliger castle and the Sigurtà Park. Near Peschiera, in the village of Pastrengo, is the Living Nature Park.

P. 61. Peschiera, view of the
harbour from over the tennis courts

Peschiera, views of the canal

Peschiera, vessels on the Mincio,
the outlet of Garda

Peschiera, "I Bastioni", the
fortifications on the harbour

Peschiera, view of the quay

Peschiera, Sanctuary
of Madonna del Frassino

LAKE of GARDA

Layout: PUBBLIEMME NEW
Photography: DI GIOVINE PHOTOGRAFICA
TIZIANA GAMBARETTO - UMBERTO PERETTI
GIORGIO PELLATI
The publisher wishes to thank the A.P.T. of Brescia for its kind
permission to reproduce the photograph on page 14

Text: ANGELO PERETTI

Printed: March 1993

STORTI EDIZIONI Casella Postale 361, 30170 MESTRE-VENEZIA (ITALIA)